PERI DWYER WORRELL

Breathe Together

Conspiracy and other poems of the plague year

First published by Eupocalypse Books 2025

Second edition

ISBN (paperback): 978-1-962454-00-1
ISBN (hardcover): 978-1-962454-07-0

This book was professionally typeset on Reedsy.
Find out more at reedsy.com

Contents

Preface

Also by Peri Dwyer Worrell

Novels:
    The Eupocalypse Trilogy:
    Machine Sickness
    Watch It Burn
    Catallaxis

Sea of Lies

Short Stories:
    No Cook, Mystery Weekly
    Tongue, Aggregate
    On Good Authority, After Dinner Conversation
    The Butcher's Dog, Wyldblood Magazine and
    Hiraeth, Shelter of Daylight

Poetry:
    Plexus, Tiny Seed
    Verge, Westerly
    We Both Know That Ain't True, Dime Show Review
    Things You Learn, Prospectus

1

Taming What Infests Us

Originally published in Crack the Spine

Invaded, a pouch, a crease, a sulcus
  Tiny entities that do not matter do
  Matter now that they have bred
  Though you never took them in.

Nothing to do now but love them
  A boy in a tenement's pets
  Six legs, racing roaches in jars
  Pigeons, rats, mitochondria.

Here, parrots flock and strip
  Fruit from the trees and sing
  In cages on the porch. Know
  What's yours is never and always theirs.

2

Safe in the Sunshine

originally published in The Five Two

The sun, the breeze, the waves.
  Something solid, and beneath,
  The shade and further back, the
  Dark pain and rage from times
  Long past, dealt with, beat back.
  Surge now in swift attack,
  A venal, manly moan, I
  Shower salt water from my hair,
  You burst right in, you whine.
  At once my rage wakes up
  As though no time has passed:
  My dad, my mom, the bath,
  Her nude and dragged, the sound
  As feet slip in the tub,
  A groan of things that slide
  Out of control like feet,
  Like fists, a face, a fall.
  And all the blows mom took,
  Black eyes, bruised, stiff neck.

Sun shone in through the bars
On windows to keep us safe
And who stayed safe?
Who? Who?
The monsters live within.

3

Chiapas

originally published in Rabbit

Tiered red blooms on branching trees.
   Green sharp mountains: dragon spine.
   Lakes: their plunge a power source.

Water that courses down
   Arroyos past block homes
   With no power lines to block
   The view and tanks on trucks
   To bring them water in dry
   December, when each trickle in itself
   Is nothing. Nothings add up
   To something when el Sumidero
   Claims the drops, gathers them
   Like chia seeds (yes, chia) and pours
   Them down cascades, then bears
   Them to the Gulf. There they drain
   Into the bays, flow out
   Into the sea past
   Platforms of grey steel

Where orange-suited men pull up the oil
That runs the trucks that transport
Water up the hills to wet the lips
Of children chasing chickens in
Dry
Winter
Dust.

4

Schrödinger's Baby

Did you think of abortion? No.
  Flooded with tears, hormones, but more:
  Relief from the sorrow you felt
  From years of trying and finding
  That profound act denied you.
  You would never.
  No.

Did you see it? Yes.
  The waves above sound revealed
  The black and white particles of a tiny bean
  Inside a bubble, inside a bowl.
  A box containing someone that wasn't, won't be, is, will be.

Did the ultrasound show a heartbeat? No.
  The probe going back and forth, back and forth,
  The doctor played the footage once again,
  Over and over, listening for the sound
  Which might be there,
  Or might have been something else.

Did the doctor seem worried? No.
    It's early yet for you.
    It will be clear in time. You are one
    Of many women whose future spreads out ahead,
    Women trailing behind in the doctor's past.
    Delivered, or not.

Are your cycles unpredictable? Yes.
    All cycles are.

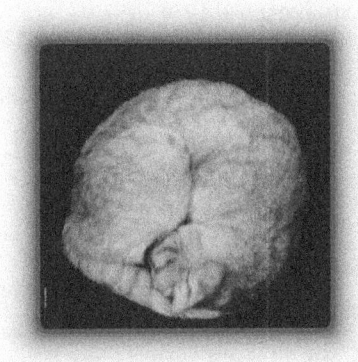

5

Cavernosa

Into the earth we enter
  Casting crumbs of light to make a
  trail
  back
  home.
  Our brightest bulbs like endoscopes illuminate
  Tiny details of stone anatomy:
  throat, vulva, pulmonic valve, renal calyx.
  Pools of liquid, dark streaks in the wall.
  And silently we come to know
  We're superficial, never deep at all.

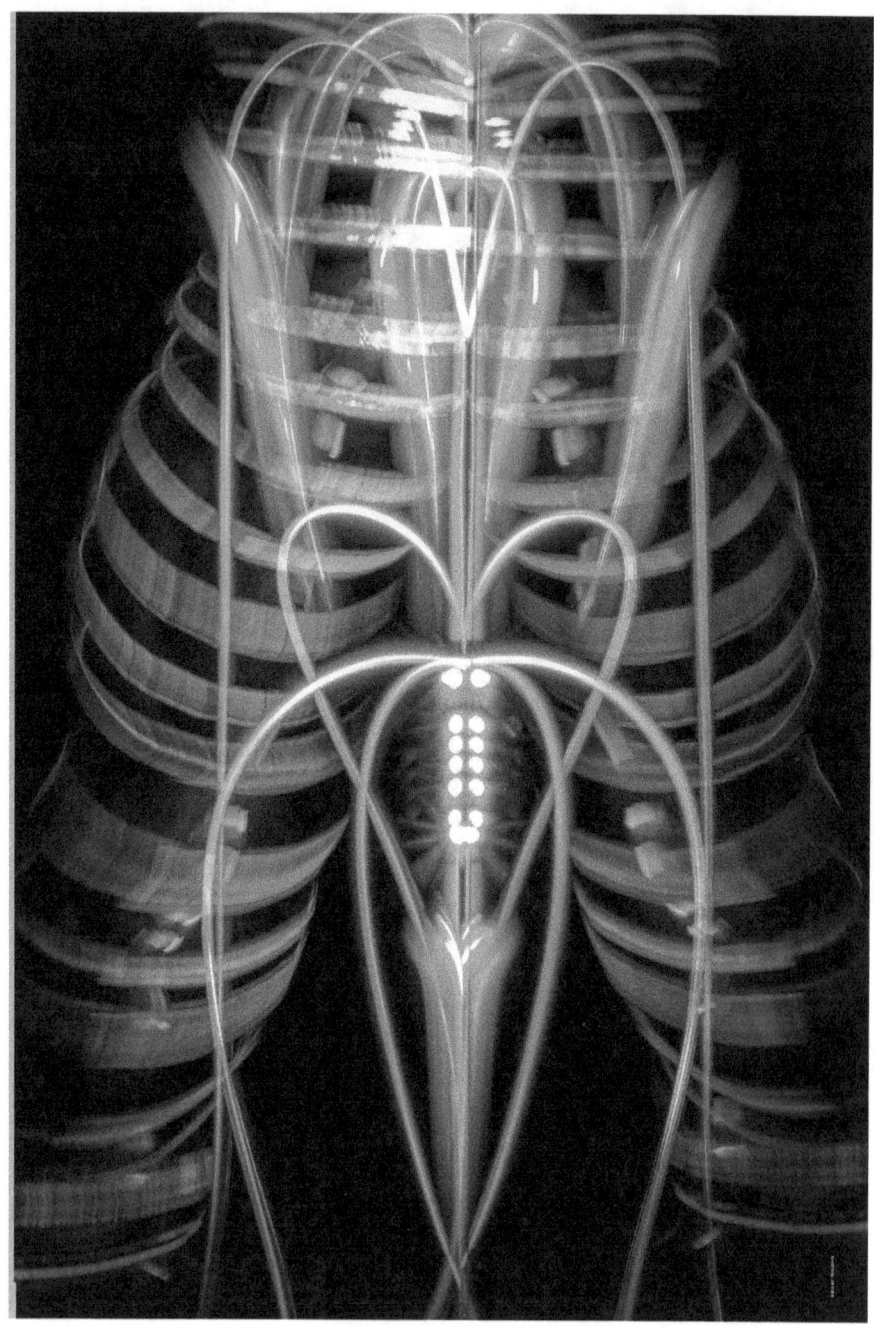

6

Breath and Gravity

Tender gravity, constant companion, never failing,
  Shaping our hearts and ever reminding us to note
  Our foundations, our cores, shaping our bones,
  Framing the very breath inside pliable ribs.

Breath, sound, sustenance, that one thing we can't
  Live without. Respire fast, respire deep, sigh out slow,
  Breathe in fragrant kindness with each breath,
  Let it saturate your one and only heart.

Heart, broken open, broken, shattered and rebuilt,
  Pulsing compassion through our chests, pumping
  Nourishment to each body's soft and living cells,
  Sending wisdom to warm our distant brains.

Brain, thought, iridescent crystal form in space,
  Not-space. Source of song, seat of sight, dancing light,
  And thoughts of dread. Computing laws
  Of nature, gravity, entropy, seeing causal chains.

7

The Spring They Stole

I walked into the station to report a theft
  Can I describe the item stolen? Why, yes:
  Days of medium length. Light winds off the ocean.
  Breezes outdoors in the sun with friends.

Identifying features?
  Faith in free expression, common sense.
  My grandson's first kick.
  The sound of music while walking down the street.
  A future for my family: work, play, hugs, joy.

The worst part of the robbery
  Was when I shouted "Stop! Thief!"
  And the cops threw a blanket on my head
  And thumped me until I stopped shouting.

Hearts attacked, hearts broken. Hours and days tick on.
  There's no "pause" button as we all stop, fatten, ache,
  Spend dazed hours waiting on electronic deposits
  That never come. Of course, there's no one on the phones.

No one can deduce the curve.
    Nothing's flat except our affect.
    No one knows what's being measured,
    Changing from centimeters to ounces
    While moving the endpoint of the tape.
    And somehow the Spring they stole
    Was taken voluntarily at gunpoint
    Because we were more afraid of dying
    Than of not living. Death just grins and waits
    Somewhere past the end of stolen Spring.

8

Conspiracy

A Panic in Seven Breaths

1. Sharing Breath

Life support training
   Is mandatory.
   The rulebook says so.
   Human Relations confirms
   The touch of death may come at any time.
   We can only avert the chill by
   Breathing together,
   taking the weight
   Of moving air in
   For someone who briefly
   Can't.

Kneel.
   Obeisant.
   Worship the plastic life

Surrogate, the thing but not
The thing itself.
Tilt back the head.
Blow into the inert mouth.
It won't breathe
With you—
Pretend.
The chest
Collapses
With each thrust
In vain.
There is
No heart.

And the glowing screen?
Sit. Look at faces, filtered.
Hear voices, manipulated.
Don't speak too fast or loud
Or the band will narrow,
The face pixelate.
You'll be left hearing voices,
Confused, trying to connect.
But there's no need
To do CPR
When the icy hand lands on your shoulder.

2. Risking Exposure

The strange thing is
when you have done nothing wrong
you still have everything to lose.

If you have nothing to hide,
you have everything to fear.
If you have not stolen secrets
Then you don't know the truth.
What's the truth worth to you?
Is it worth as much to them?
Truth lies in the gutter.
Pick it up, brush it off.
Don't let anyone see you.
Masks were forbidden
Until they were mandatory.
The best type of mask
Makes you suck.
If you stay still and silent you're fine.
If you are active it
Slowly lowers your O2
Until you can't
Think.

If you speak, you are unheard
   Unless you shout.
   If you shout, you are irrational,
   Angry, irresponsible.
   Since you can't think you need
   To be taught how to think.
   But first: put on the mask.

Hide the face
   Of the beast,
   The face
   Of your one true love,
   Your mother's face,
   The face

Of loss.

You don't get to choose
    what to risk.
    Heartfelt activity?
    Too much risk.
    Inactive activism,
    Checked for orthodoxy.
    Lip service to the oppressed
    Is that lip smiling?
    Or does it sneer?
    No one knows.

Dive.
    Retreat to safe
    caves under water
    where you can't breathe
    Without a mask,
    Without a tube
    Connecting you to filtered air
    That whispers in your face,
    The face no one
    Can see.

4. Lives

The crime is this:
    the knee
    On our necks is not the root cause.
    The cause is hearts that broke
    A long time ago, but momentum

Kept us going until
All meaning fled our lives.

There was: a virus,
  meth, and fentanyl
  in his system.
  There was false money in the system,
  False money in his hand.
  False news, false outrage.
  Real breath
  that stopped.
  We are not all him,
  We can breathe.
  We can breathe alone
  But we can't breathe together,
  We can't con
  spire
  Not in theory,
  Not in truth.

5. Building Rapport During the Interview

If you want to get at the truth,
  mirror the subject's movements.
  Touch your face when he does
  (Don't touch your face)
  Lean in when she does
  (Don't get too close)
  When s/he sighs, you sigh
  (You breathe together).
  Respect boundaries,

Create consent
(But don't shake hands).
Watch your mouth;
No one else can.

6. Air Passages

Whisper
    through loose throat
    Shapes that hiss, sculpted
    From trickles deep inside
    But moved by muscle
    thrusting deep below.

Sing.
    Emanate the music
    Throughout the room,
    diffusing joy.
    This stream of air
    Focused on a spot
    Strung tight within your throat
    Aerosol of sound,
    Uplifted voice.
    Unite in
    Hymns of joy,
    Paeans of praise,
    Raps of rage,
    Rhythm and blues,
    A cappella harmonies.

Orate if you must,

But remember every phrase
Is driven by that hunk
Of flesh that presses
A million tiny chambers
Webbed with blood,
Sucks through ten
Thousand tiny straws
With greed that won't give up
Its life. It's life.

Scream!
Shriek alarm.
Take precedence.
Each cave in your chest
Home to the virus
Vibrates with the strength
Of everything you've ever said.
Too bad
It's muffled
In a mask.

7. Story

The lede lies
Bleeding.
The figures fall
Down memory holes.
Computer models based
On suspect assumptions,
Suspects assumed to have died
In botched robberies,

Suicides, assassinations.
Foil hats, face shields.
And once again, masks.
Yellow vests,
Color revolutions,
Black lives,
White supremacy,
Thin blue lines,
Withdrawal from occupied nations,
Pilate washing his hands.

The curve is flat, the Earth is flat.

Did you think you would never die?

9

Sunlight

Sunlight
   Cleanse, bronze, heal me.
   Kiss my whiteness gently.
   You, above all others, know I'm
   Fragile.

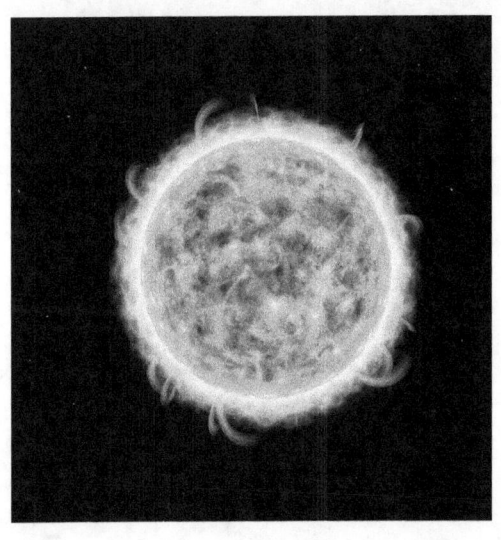

10

Geothermal

Earth's magma lunges for the sun
  Pours, spills, wells up and overflows.
  An infant's heart that wailed for mom's,
  Bubbled up, boiled over and hissed.
  Now, suckle. Sweetness, ease,
  Comfort and cradled sleep
  (Breeze and cloud, plant and beast),
  And wake prepared to gaze
  Into her eyes, too bright by far,
  Our need too great for us to bear.
  The faintest touch on thinnest skin,
  Neutrinos flying through unfelt
  Our future flying towards us,
  A comet we adore in awe
  And never live to see again.

11

Playa Plague

I chose to seek the shining sun,
  Forget cold feet, ice, and freezing rain,
  Leave my home with naked arms each day
  To kiss the sea breeze from the white sand

When life came to a screeching halt
  (Collective panic, now all's said and done)
  Panting birds flew streets with open beaks
  To kiss the sea breeze from the white sand.

Locals fled illness to their tiny towns.
  The threat of death was worth financial pain.
  Leaving us in masks, alone, to yearn
  To kiss the sea breeze from the white sand.

Silent, sun-dried, masked, I am just one
  Who longs to raise my arms to postponed rain.

12

Wake

You try to free yourself
    But you only hurt your wrist.
    Torn apart joint by joint.
    You hear a loud bang!
    You're not torn apart, but
    Turned into someone else.

Reunited forever with
    Everyone you've ever loved;
    You'll never see them again.
    You're in a box of water
    That's not a box and has
    No water in it.

You drown anyway.

13

Positive Pressure

Maybe it was when we stopped breathing together,
  When you set up the machine that hummed in your face,
  Wrapped yourself in tubes that took you away from me,
  So I wore earplugs which put me in a separate world,
  Away from your wet lips on my dry hair, your arm
  Across my back, my foot between your calves, warm,
  Satisfying, cleaving you to me and making us. Perhaps
  There are worse things than apnea, like loneliness.

We'd stopped breathing as one. I'd started yoga class instead.
  You'd roll your eyes when I picked up the mat to go.
  I stood and breathed with strangers, the heat making me stream wet;
  You'd go out to the bar and tell your friends I left you
  All alone, wave thousand-peso bills, red flags to brittle girls
  Who never learned to breathe, who always had their breasts
  Thrust and bobbing atop a coy, cinched center full of fear.

Then the world stopped. We watched it lose its mind,
  Breathing separately. Your eyes ceased to focus, your words
  Cruel, hissing indefensible rage then staring into space, aloof

For hours, then forgetting we had spoken at all. But years
Had passed since we entwined all night, lovers and beloveds,
The loss I felt, explored, delved, channeled into art,
The loss you felt subsumed only into blame, escaped
With alcohol and furtive lust, panting falsely, truly fucked.

14

Non Sequitur

What might the gunman say
  If you asked him for the time?
  Don't you think he'd pause and
  Answer you truthfully?

What might the cat think of the carrot?

Yesterday's lottery numbers
  Want so hard to be cared about.
  It's a difficult desire.

15

Grand

My eyes crinkle but that's how
    They move, each time I smile now.
    Your eyes are still so smooth and bright.
    Fresh eyes will open on the light.
    Your hopes, realized, your flawless plans
    Destroyed. Just create all-new plans,
    Your life diverted off its course,
    Switched by unfathomable force,
    By gentle love, by power untold:
    One tiny dot inside you rolled
    Into that cradle we thought sere
    And barren, but right now, right here,
    You are one of a million today,
    Today you are a single ray
    Of light. You beam through the black
    Velvet of infinity whose back
    Is hope, wonder, fear, and dread.
    The emergence of that little head,
    So small! And yet so huge! The pain
    I felt that day for you, insane
    Agony, joy, shock, hope, regret.

Irrevocable, you choose to make the bet
You'll lose, for life is full of grief
And furious changes, time a thief,
Gravity, relentless, is your foe,
And that which is precious will go
The way of evil, joy the way
Of pain, night merging into day.
But you, you whom I would give all,
Chose to leap. I can only watch you fall
In love with one who's flesh of flesh.
And see you start the world afresh.

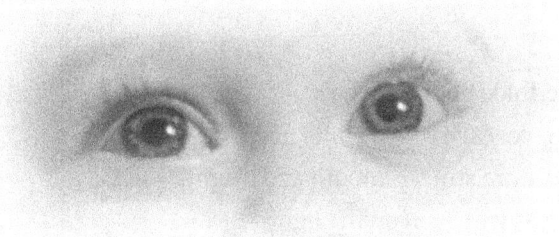

16

Undreaming the Nightmare

Wake heart pounding, mouth dry, palms sweating
  Did you gasp and pant?
  Silence of the stolen springtime
  just a dream fumbling for the light
  your face full of holes, nails raking itching lumps off your arms feet
  belly
  A simple explanation
  Pasted your 6th grade essay into it by mistake
  Pics of your man thigh to thigh with her (your friends laugh with
  them)
  struggling to wake fully, fighting to ban the image from your eyes
  Surely the deserted streets and locked doors were a fluke
  Did they really pull your essay down?
  Closed airports, roadblocks one at a time to buy food no didn't really
  happen
  the light was already on
  Didn't pay your hosting fee.
  trying to reach a doctor
  the police would never send you home
  You misread the first line (and the rest)
  it was just for a day or two, not months

you were not in bed at all
It was all a misunderstanding.
Someone else wrote spoofed drivel under your name
How confusing these things are! Who could explain why?
Three years on, still rage.

Vertigo
Breathe
Never done
Breathe
This is what they really are
Shout into a well
Breathe
Say it
Say it again
Demand it back
Breathe
Clutch it tight
Make it right
Turn on the light

Bonus material: Short story

The Butcher's Dog

Originally published in
Wyldblood

He sold me, but I'm sure it
was a mistake.

I sat erect under the
corrugated metal roof over the
Mercado 28 de Febrero in
Cuenca, Ecuador. All the other
market dogs dropped their
tails, curled their ears, and
slunk around me –
and quite rightly. I barely
even acknowledged them (unless
there was a bitch in heat, of
course). Why should I? My
sleek fur and soft contours
clearly demonstrated my
superiority, in contrast to
their dull coats and gaunt
ribs.

My privilege and dignity were
due to my loyal, loving, and
natural devotion to Hector,
the butcher. The booth I
guarded at night was set up
each morning, filled with
delectable whole chickens,
pigs' sides hung on hooks

above the swine's heads on the
counter, and heaps of
scrumptious ground beef. For
breakfast, I lapped blood from
the concrete before it
disappeared down the drain in
the floor. I nabbed scraps of
skin and fat that flew when
the cleaver whacked flesh on
the gouged and stained wood
block.
The customers came day in and
day out: stocky, serious
indigenas buying chickens
complete with feet and head;
restaurateurs who'd buy an
entire half pig and minutely
oversee the cuts; every now
and then a rich *gringa* who'd
demand all fat be trimmed
away, the feet and heads
discarded. The last were my
favorite.
Hector took their money and
gave them their meat. One day,
instead of meat, he took a
man's money and instead of
meat, he gave him me.
Perhaps I should explain my
background. First, I'm of a
herding breed. Think of a
border collie, or an

Australian shepherd. Then think of generations of my ancestors weaving our way through the untidy traffic of Andean towns. The dullards among us don't survive to breed. I don't mean to brag, here. It's just a simple statement of fact that we're among the smartest dogs in the world.

My mother was in charge of herding an entire rural flock, mixed goats and alpacas. It was poetry in motion to watch her agility as she guided them along the steepest ravines, or expertly cut the very one the owner desired out of the flock. One morning well before dawn, when I was not yet a year old, I pranced along at the heels of the herder's son one morning. He was on his way to sell fat goats for slaughter.

The meat wholesaler, Raul, eyed me with admiration. His gaze kept falling on me during his preliminary small talk with the youth. I stared back.

I followed the transactions
easily, watching hands and
faces, nods and body language,
smelling the puffs of social
pheromones. When their
business was done, it was
clear that I'd been part of
the transaction. I licked the
boy's hand, once only, and
crossed to lie down at the
meat distributor's feet. But
that ownership was brief.
Around sunrise, I trotted out
of the warehouse, a few inches
behind the left heel of the
next customer. He was a retail
butcher — Hector. Raul threw
me in on a bargain that Hector
had pressed him hard on.
No need to be indignant! this
happens to pups, at least the
worthy ones among us who
aren't driven out into the
streets or thrown off cliffs
in burlap bags. This is a poor
country, and pets are a
luxury.
I followed Hector to Raul's
loading dock, where I sat
silently, ears forward.
Watching him supervise the
carcasses loaded on his truck,

I assessed him as forthright, calm, and fair. He struck me an alpha with nothing to prove. His body odor bespoke moderation but not abstention. I approved of the man. I was content with my fate.

When loading finished, at a nod from Hector, I jumped into the truck's cab and took my place on the passenger-side floorboard.

That first glorious day at the mercado, I could hardly believe my luck! At dusk, we returned to Hector's home, a walled compound of wooden buildings on stilts, set into a hillside. His children ran up squealing to meet the new dog. After ear-scratching and hand-licking, I investigated a hutch of cuys, little edible rodents that they kept for holiday meat. Hector's wife eyed me warily as I sniffed the free-ranging chickens until she was satisfied that I wouldn't kill one. When it got cold that night, I found a warm spot next to the kitchen wall where the fire was banked

in the corner and curled up
for the night.
I was home.
#
But when this event of which I
speak happened, I was five
years old, already in love
with Hector, proud of my place
in the market at his feet,
reveling in the daily
carnivorous feast, basking in
the sunshine in the thin
mountain air. I felt sure I
was set for life.
Then the gringo Charlie walked
into the *mercado*. I knew him
as a regular customer,
smelling, as usual, like too
much mint and not enough
garlic, combined with a
chemical disinfectant smell I
intensely disliked. Today he
also smelled just recovered
from a cold, overlaid with the
lovely funky sweat of recent
sex. Visually, he looked soft
and pale, as always, and he
laughed his normal, harshly
nervous laugh that set my neck
hairs twitching. However, I
ignored the laugh and wagged
my tail, drooling, because he

usually pinched off a tiny piece of ground meat and flicked it to me right after Hector weighed it. He picked out his meats for the week and spoke intently with Hector. I gave a tiny yip of surprise when I realized by their looks at me and their body language, the smells of Hector's reluctance and greed and the gringo's determination and triumph, that I was part of today's deal.

When it was done, Charlie clicked his tongue.

"Mashi," he called me. I followed, stiff-legged, looking repeatedly back at Hector, expecting him to change his mind, but he ignored me. The smell of his regret was the only goodbye I got.

To add insult to injury, when I walked past the seamstress's booth down the aisle, the fragrance of my distress emboldened her creepy little dachshund. He darted out and nipped at my hind leg, an impudence he'd never have

tried the day before. I
snarled and pinned him with a
paw. His yips and growls
attracted everyone's
attention. The seamstress
whipped a scrap of velvet at
us, and he scrambled back.
Charlie grabbed my scruff and
spoke sternly to me in
English. He slipped a collar
around my neck and clipped a
leash to it, the first time
I'd ever been bound. I shook
my head and backed up, but
finding myself captive, I
followed him. This did not
bode well for my future.
Charlie took me to his home, a
second-floor suite facing the
courtyard of a colonial
building. I lived indoors, an
odd arrangement. We went out
every day for a walk in the
neighborhood. I didn't
understand the English words
of his commands at first, but
his meaning was usually clear.
"Sit" was "*siéntete,*" for
example.
He'd walk with me each morning
to the city park, cautioning
me to "Stay… Stay…. Stay,"

every few seconds, until
finally...

"Go!" I would spring forward
and race up and down the
grassy meadows. Charlie would
ignore me. I would pause on a
small rise at the end of the
park closest to the *mercado*,
sniffing the air for all the
smells there, but especially
for the meat smell. When I
caught that iron blood aroma,
I examined it for the
slightest trace of Hector's
familiar odor.

I found out that Charlie's
chemical smell was
concentrated in a room at the
end of his suite. He entered
it only after donning booties,
plastic gloves, a coverall,
and a plastic face shield.
When Charlie went in there, I
lay across the doorway and
waited, sometimes for hours of
solitude and boredom. I was
trying to be a good dog for
Charlie, but I missed Hector.
#
One day, we came home from our
early-morning walk and Charlie
disappeared into the room. He

came out after a short time
holding a syringe.
"Here you go, boy!" he said. I
wagged my tail, since that was
his phrase when he tossed me a
scrap. But instead he knelt,
pinched up the skin on my
neck, and injected me with the
syringe. "You're officially
CRISPRed!" He gave his jerky
laugh.
I felt odd immediately. My
heart beat faster and I felt
like I might vomit. I stumbled
to my plush bed in the corner
and lay down.
I slept the rest of the day;
it was twilight when I
awakened. My throat was sore
and my nose was dry. I shook
my head and immediately
regretted it as the room spun.
I reeled to my water bowl and
lapped up so much water that I
did vomit a little, which hurt
my sore throat terribly.
Charlie stood over me, writing
in a notebook. I collapsed on
my belly then, and after a few
minutes he scooped me up and
carried me back to my bed.

I stayed in that bed for a few days, turning up my nose at the meals Charlie put in front of me, often putting my paws over my eyes to block the painful daylight, my ears folded to block the normal city sounds, now acutely amplified. A couple of times, Charlie disturbed me to draw blood from my foreleg, but that barely registered through the fog of pain and nausea. Eventually I began to feel better. One morning, I still had a dull headache, but I was ravenously hungry. I walked over to my untouched meal from the day before, chicken offal, *mote*, and broth, and began to eat.

What a strange sensation as I worked my tongue and teeth! As a dog, I had no lips to speak of, but my mouth muscles quivered oddly around my jowls and chin. When I swallowed, something in my throat I'd never felt before quivered. Charlie noticed I was up. "You're eating, Mashi! Good boy!" I beat my tail on the floor. "Is that good, Mashi? Is it good?"

As spontaneously as my tail wagged, I raised my head and made a noise. It wasn't exactly a bark.

"Goooo," I said.

Charlie's eyebrows shot up. His smell signaled excitement. He grabbed his notebook and scribbled something.

"Mashi." My tail thumped again. "Is that…*goooooood*?" he drew out the sounds carefully and my eyes were drawn to his mouth.

My mouth and throat seemed out of my control as I formed the syllable back at him, "Gooooo." I was unequipped for the "d" sound so I ended the word with a short, shrill yip.

"Yes!" Charlie made a fist and did a little dance. My tail thumped. Suddenly I was exhausted again. I walked to my bed and collapsed, leaving Charlie to scribble.

#

As I regained my health, we resumed our daily walks. I gradually built my endurance

back up in the park. I never
stopped pausing on the rise,
and now I tried to form the
sounds of his name, "Hector"
as I sniffed the breeze.
I regained the weight I'd
lost, though my coat was never
as lush as it had been when I
was the butcher's dog, king of
the *mercado*.
Charlie grew irritable. Mainly
it seemed, he was angry that
he couldn't tell anyone about
me.
"Mashi," tail thump, "they
wouldn't understand, would
they, boy?" He'd scratch my
ears. "But you're the proof
aren't you? Might even outlive
me, won't you? And you're a
real best friend, aren't you a
real best friend?"
"Veshk ren(yip)," I'd answer.
Best friend. Each time I tried
to make a phoneme my mouth was
unsuited for, I got a little
closer. But a full nasal stop
while voicing was still tricky
for me. And my changing face
refused to grow lips.
Now, dogs don't lie. That's
part of why people love dogs,

I think. But a really smart dog, such as, for example, a herding breed that's been naturally selected for cunning over generations, can mislead, withhold information, or redirect.

I quickly realized that Charlie thought I understood no more language than I could speak. But the truth was, slowly as my body was changing and allowing me to approach intelligible speech, my brain was outpacing it exponentially.

"We'll just have to repeat the blood test a little earlier this week, won't we?" Charlie would muse. A lonely man, he spoke to me a lot. I let him think it was in the nature of talking to himself, but inside my head I was thinking, *you'll probably do it Tuesday instead of Thursday because you're seeing Elena on Thursday this week, aren't you? And Wednesday is your cards night.* "We'll do it Tuesday. Yes, we will. Who's my good boy?" Tail thump. "Is it Mashi? Is Mashi a good, good boy?"

"Goo(yip) oy." *Good boy.* I walked up to him for an ear rub, but he was already engrossed in his computer. I missed Hector.

#

Then came the day Charlie drew blood from my foreleg, then followed it up with an injection that made me fall asleep.

I woke inside a small box with mesh windows. The latch was a simple mechanism. Charlie knew by now that I was smart and determined enough to undo most latches, limited only by my lack of thumbs, so he'd added a combination lock.

The box was inside a vehicle, an SUV, and Charlie sat next to the driver. I lay quietly and watched the sky on one side and cliff faces on the other as we wended our way down switchbacks. A few times I spotted alpacas and thought nostalgically of my mother. Finally, after descending many thousands of feet in altitude,

the road straightened out onto
Ecuador's coastal plateau.
In another hour or two, we
stopped at a busy location
(which I now know was an
airport). At the time, the
smell of aviation fuel,
thousands of people from all
over, the ocean breeze, and
the glorious stink of the city
of Guayaquil were
overwhelming, strange and new.
I stood inside the crate,
yearning to get out to
explore, but instead a
stranger loaded the crate on a
cart and left me to sit in the
unfamiliar equatorial heat for
hours.
I was eventually loaded into
the belly of a plane. The
noise was incredible,
reminding me of those first
post-CRISPR days when my head
felt like it would burst. But
soon the air became thin and
dry and cold again, like
Cuenca, and I settled into an
uneasy sleep.
I'll skip the transition
through Customs and the trip
to Charlie's house. Suffice it

to say, I was confused and withdrawn during the whole ordeal and for days afterwards.

Charlie's home was huge by Ecuadorian standards, though I gathered from comments he made on the phone to his friends and family that it was normal for the US. I disliked the laminate floors in the living area intensely, for both their plasticky odor and the way my toenails scraped on them, so I spent as much time as I could on the kitchen tile or in the carpeted bedrooms.

But the wonderful thing about Charlie's American home was that it had a backyard that opened onto a power-line easement that stretched for miles! Several times a day, I'd stand by the back door.

"Run!" I'd say.

"You want to run? You want to run? Sit!" Charlie would reach for the doorknob. I'd obediently sit, quivering with anticipation.

"Stay!" he'd say, while he opened the door.

I'd freeze.
"Go, Mashi! Run!"
I'd dash out the door, pause
to work the latch on the back
gate, and race for miles up
and down under the power
lines. Sometimes I'd meet a
human jogger, try to herd a
giggling group of children
playing, or chase a cat
briefly. I'd encounter other
dogs and we'd butt-sniff, play
bow, and run back and forth a
few times, but as a herding
breed, I wasn't as much of a
pack animal as most dogs. But
there are no words for the joy
I felt in running as fast as I
could, as far as I wanted. In
those moments, I was free from
the strangeness of the
creature I'd become, no longer
dog, not quite person.
  I was also free of the
deception of pretending to be
stupider than I am.
Finally, Charlie would put two
fingers in his mouth and
whistle. I might be miles away
by then, but I'd hear, turn,
and race back.

I think those runs were all
that saved me from losing my
mind.

Charlie worked as an
independent laboratory safety
consultant (ironic,
considering how many
regulations he'd violated by
performing his CRISPR on me).
His various contracts around
the Dallas area where we lived
often required him to go to
work every day for weeks or
months, but the rest of the
time, he spoke with other
humans by phone, if at all.
In Ecuador, he'd been forced
to visit the crowded *mercados*
for food, and he'd had a
weekly card game with other
English-speaking expats. He'd
even had an Ecuadorian
girlfriend, though her
pregnancy (I could smell that
the baby was his, but he
didn't believe it. I remained
tactfully silent on the
matter) was what precipitated
our sudden move. But here, he
ordered groceries and anything
he needed online, including a

call girl every couple of
weeks.
I was the only one he spoke
to, many days.
"Good boy, Mashi! Is he a good
boy?"
"Goo(yip) oy!" I'd respond.
"Here's a cookie!" He'd give
me a treat, one of the fishy,
brothy-tasting crisps I loved.
I understood what he was
doing. *Two can play at that
game,* I thought.
One day while he was at work,
I dragged a runner from the
carpeted bedroom to the
detestable laminate floor.
When Charlie came home, after
he'd let me out for my run, he
moved the rug back where it
had come from.
"Who's a good boy?" Charlie
asked expectantly.
I stood looking at him,
wagging my tail.
"Who's a *good boy*?" he asked,
slower and louder.
I clicked my poor toenails
across that heinous laminate
to the bedroom and stood,
looking at him, next to the
runner. He followed me.

"Who's a good boy?" He tried
again. I slowly wagged my tail
but didn't move, holding his
gaze, summoning the alpha
authority of my days as king
of the *mercado*.
Slowly, it dawned on him. He
picked up the runner and put
it back, forming a bridge
across the clicky, smelly
laminate so I could cross from
carpet to tile without
touching it. I marched proudly
across the bridge and stood by
my food bowl.
"Goo(yip) oy!" I said.
#
Training Charlie went well
after that. Some things he
knew I was teaching him to do,
like leaving a few treats on
the counter so I could help
myself when he was at work.
"Treats." I pointed at the
counter with my nose. Once he
figured out what I wanted, he
seemed amused. I rewarded him
with a new vocabulary word
each time.
"Chair," I'd say, hopping on
and off the kitchen chair.

"Ook," nudging an open book on the coffee table.

Other behaviors took longer to reinforce, because he had no idea he was doing them.

Leaving his computer logged into voice command mode, for example. I had to wait for him to enable it, which he only did occasionally. Then I chattered my way through all my vocabulary words and tossed in a few new ones. It took three or four months of that, and about forty new words, before he started leaving voice command on all the time. After that, it took a number of redirection strategies before he got in the habit of leaving it on in the morning when he went to work.

Now I was cooking, as they say. Though, no, I never felt any urge to learn to cook. Dogs are almost without exception raw-foods enthusiasts. Cooking smells are just a signal to us that humans are handling food and we'd better get in there and get our share.

I always feel the urge to learn, though. And in an era of instant e-learning online, a talking dog with a voice-activated computer is all set. There was a bit of a learning curve on the computer's part while it learned to deal with my, shall we say, idiosyncratic accent. And there was a panicked near-miss one afternoon when the garage door opened and I almost didn't get the web browser shut down in time.

After that, I started a program of talking more, immediately on his entry, when he took a long time to get out of the car and come inside. That was such a subtle behavior to reinforce it took many months to noticeably slow his transition time. After a year or so, though, he was consistently sitting in the car and sipping a beverage, flipping through social media on his phone, before coming inside.

Much less stressful for me.

By the time I turned eight, I was talking with Charlie using the vocabulary of a bright three-year-old human. I had finished 6th-grade math and introductory computer science, and worked my way, backwards, through world history to the 6th century on Chan Academy. I had several e-mail accounts. Being, as previously mentioned, thumbless, I had to wait with vigilance and patience for Charlie to leave his credit card lying out, but by that time I had fair control over how much he drank each evening. When he laid the card down by the keyboard and poured himself a scotch, it was a simple matter of tail wags, nudges, licks, a couple of new words, and so forth to lead him to drink seven or eight of them. He staggered to bed and fell in with his clothes on, so I dragged the quilt over him to make sure he'd sleep soundly. Then I went back and memorized the card information, front and back. I carefully replaced the card where he'd left it.

As I surfed online more, I began to look at Charlie's wardrobe critically. Though he had PhD in biochemistry, and seemed to have adequate clientele, I could tell that he was pushing the boundaries of acceptable attire: worn flip-flops, chinos that were faded and frayed. Here in the USA, home of giant portions and sugary drinks and snacks, his polo shirts had begun to stretch across his belly unflatteringly. I burrowed into his closet and drawers, exhuming shirts in larger sizes, loafers, and dress socks, laboriously repacking his wardrobe so they were a little more accessible. Occasionally, I even dragged a particularly threadbare or tight garment out to the trash barrel when he was at work on trash pick-up day, though I risked one of the neighbors noticing and mentioning it to him. I logged onto his user accounts and searched for

hours for business-casual
clothing so he'd be inundated
with ads for dressier
trousers. His ad feed was now
full of photos of men posing
gazing off the pier in
yachting clothes, or standing
by a big desk in a corner
office in crisp professional
attire. Then, one night, I
made a real sacrifice to
achieve my goals: I chewed up
his flip-flops.
I won't lie: I enjoyed it. I
am a dog, and the combined
flavors and aromas of leather,
rubber, and toe jam were
scrumptious. But, unlike
stupider dogs, I fully
understood that I would be
scolded and punished for it. I
may be a standoffish herding
dog, but I *am* a dog, and being
yelled at and having my nose
smacked, followed by being
locked in my crate, was an
emotionally difficult
experience for me, even
knowing that it was for a good
cause.
But my sacrifice was rewarded
the next day when he finally

donned the loafers that I'd
tugged just far enough out of
the back-bottom corner of the
closet so that he could spot
them. Now I had a master whose
appearance I could at least be
somewhat proud of, even if he
was an unethical, awkward
boor.

It made me miss Hector even
more: Hector, the butcher, the
don of the mercado, a true
caballero, respected by the
indigenas in their velvet
skirts, beloved by all the
almond-eyed children, so
respected he was sometimes
asked to mediate petty
disputes. Hector, always
forthright, always upright,
and always kind.

One day I was out on my run
when I caught the whiff of a
bitch in heat. It had been a
long time for me, and this one
had a healthy aroma. My nose
took over my body, my mind
along for the ride, and I
veered to the smell's source.
Which was an eight-foot
privacy fence segregating a
yard from the power-line

easement. For a dog of my
agility, all it took was a
running start. I leapt in the
air, fully committed. My feet
scrabbled up the top few feet
of the fence, my momentum
carrying me to the top. My
front paws hooked over, my
back claws dug in…and I was in
the yard with a gorgeous
female Rottweiler. It was one
of the most joyous matings of
my life. The Rottweiler's
owner looked out her window
just as we finished and came
out, yelling, to chase me
away. The human grabbed the
Rottie's collar, causing her
sleek brown and black coat to
ripple. I grinned and simpered
against the gate, hoping to
avoid any unpleasantness. The
human let go of the bitch and
closed in on me.
"Smart one, aren't you?" she
asked.
You have no idea! I thought.
She opened the latch and I was
out. I felt relaxed,
invigorated, alive! It didn't
even dull my mood when I heard
Charlie's whistle just at that

moment. I turned my path
towards his home.

Things went on this way for
several more months. Charlie,
with his improved image, got
better clients and steadier
work. He even began to
socialize a bit, leaving me
alone longer on weekend
evenings.

I progressed in my studies,
but still I yearned for
Hector. Then I reached the
Chan Academy lessons on the
Olmec and pre-contact Andean
civilizations and my
homesickness began to throb
palpably.

It was then that I began to
formulate a plan.

So, here I am. It turned out
to be almost absurdly simple,
really. I created an online
account with a special service
for exporting pets to foreign
countries. After a thousand or
so attempts, I held a pen in
my mouth and forged my vet's
signature on the required
certificate of health. Today,
the appointed pick-up date, I
dragged my crate out onto the

porch, stacked the paperwork
neatly on a wicker loveseat,
weighted it down with a rock,
and climbed into the crate.
I'm sitting here waiting for
the transport truck to pull
up. The address for delivery
is the butcher of the *mercado*
on *Calle 28 de Febrero*,
Cuenca, Ecuador. My crate is
to be released on the
signature of one Hector.
And, to make my triumph
complete, I can smell a litter
of newborn, half-Rottweiler
puppies on the breeze.
Apparently, one of the amazing
things about CRISPR is that it
alters the germ line of future
generations. If I'm not
mistaken, the Rottweiler's
mistress will be quite taken
aback one day when she talks
to the puppies.
And they talk back.